BEND, DON'T SHATTER

poets on the beginning of desire

edited by T. Cole Rachel and Rita D. Costello

Red Rattle Books

Soft Skull Press

2004

Bend, Don't Shatter
isbn: 1-932360-17-4
© 2004 T. Cole Rachel / Rita D. Costello

First Edition
cover photographs: Joanna Ebenstein

The following poems have appeared elsewhere prior to this
anthology:

"The Boy" originally appeared in *Pavane* (Sherwood Press,
1981), © 1981, David Trinidad. Reprinted by permission of
the author.

"Slicker" originally appeared in *The World 56/57*, © 2000, David
Trinidad. Reprinted by permission of the author.

"Greyhound" originally appeared in *New Ink Journal*, Fall 1996.

"Elegy for the Hurdler" appeared in *Complaint in the Garden*,
Zoo Press.

"My Sixth Grade Sex Life: Milne Elementary, New Orleans"
appeared in *The Men in the Dark*, Lowlands Press, Stuttgart,
Germany, 2003.

"Spending the Night" appeared in *The Paris Review*, 2003, Vol.
166 (Summer), p. 213–214.

"The Odd Years" appeared in *Ignition Magazine*.

"Last Ditch" printed with permision of Four Way Books. From
The Sublimation Point by Jason Schneiderman. © 2004, Jason
Schneiderman. All rights reserved.

Published by Soft Skull Press
71 Bond Street, Brooklyn, NY 11217
www.SoftSkull.com

Distribluted by Publishers Group West
www.pgw.com | 800.788.3123
Printed in Canada

Contents

A Note from the Editors

It makes sense that most people turn to poetry during adolescence. For many of us, reading and writing poetry is a kind of therapy, especially at a time in our lives when everything is so emotionally raw. Being a teenager is confusing, and poetic language is a natural outlet for confusion. We tried to include in this book poems which show that everyone deals with this confusion–those that bully and those who are bullied, those that do well in school and those that fail, those that come from perfect homes and those who come from places not so perfect—and there is no reason to crumble under the pressure. The more comfortable you are with the uncertainty of growing up, the stronger you will be. Let the experiences—happy or terrible—make you who you are, not crush you under their weight.

It's okay not to know yet who you are or what you want, and whatever it is, you don't have to be afraid of it. We hope that these poems will let you know that other people have been there. We all have.

We hoped to make a book unlike any other that currently exists— a book that realistically deals with what it means to come of age as gay, lesbian, transgender, or, as is perhaps more often the case in adolescence, totally confused and freaked out.

So, don't worry too much. You're going to be just fine.

—*T. Cole Rachel*
Rita D. Costello

Introduction

Poetry gives us the intimate company of words and clarifies our mysteries. The poems in *Bend Don't Shatter* will pluck chords in you, chords so complex and resonant that you feel them in your spine. You'll hear truths so exact you can't explain them. But you'll sense in your bones precisely what you feel, and realize that your soul knows more than it did a minute before.

The poets in this book are writing about being young and queer. Sharing their passions and puzzles with you, they will help you discover, interpret, and corroborate who you are, who you can become, and how you can connect with other people. From Christopher Murray and David Trinidad's tender and subversive poem-stories to Andrea Shipley's sass, Scott Hightower's eloquent musings, Rigoberto González's proud and arresting lyrics, and Jody Helfand's forthright attitudes, these poets are giving voice to the queer desires we share. They write about longing for somebody and sometimes getting him or her, about being understood and misunderstood, and about struggling and coming through the other side, wiser and wised up, ready to live better and love more.

You'll see that the poems in this book cover a lot of ground, from the first glimmers of being bent to the full blossoming of our queer identities, and the ways we try to relate our queer selves to our families, our schools, our friends, and the other bodies and selves we seek. One of the big themes you'll find here is the confusion that same-sexers feel as we try to figure out the difference between infatuation and admiration—whether we really want to have someone else or be that someone else. And as its title suggests, *Bend, Don't Shatter* is not just about crying in your bedroom or negotiating the school bus when you're a girl in boy's clothes or a boy with one eye on the gymnast in the fifth row, the one who sometimes smiles back. This book tells about how you learn to become aware of your own spine and "put on your brass bra" as one friend of mine calls it, so you can advance into your world on your own terms. It's about the joy of being magnetized and propelled by desire.

Like being queer, reading poetry doesn't always come easy. In a world where images flash at you like noisy lightening, and where most people use words as blunt weapons, why should you bother with poetry's murmuring voice? A poem doesn't usually shout its meaning at you. You have to breathe it in line by line. So give these poems time. Probably you'll find yourself sparked by them into writing more poems yourself. Take the poems in this anthology as models of honesty and style, and see if you can use their strategies to translate your own truths.

Poetry has always united people. Through the words memorized by poets and recited on the hunt or around the tribal fire, our ancestors learned about their own lives and histories, and the myths, stories, and dreams that gave their lives value and significance. Today there are poetry readings and slams where people converge to share the power of the word. I hope you'll find some to go to. But when you read these poems in private, imagine all the other people reading them too. They are feeling the same things you are. They have the same questions and challenges, and they are finding solace, sense, and sustenance on the same page you are. Imagine them as your companions and confidantes. Imagine them as your tribe.

Wherever you are, read these poems aloud. If you do, they will resonate even more for you, more quickly penetrating your head as well as your heart. It feels good to hear other people's words ring out in your own voice. Speak them loud and clear—shout them if you want to. Then share them with someone else you trust. Let poetry bring you together.

—David Groff

THE BOY

Looking back,
I think that he must have been an angel.
We never spoke,
but one entire summer, every day,
he sat on the curb across the street.
I watched him: thin, his skin white,
his blond hair cut short.
Sometimes, right after swimming,
his bathing suit wet and tight,
he would sit and dry off in the sun.
I couldn't stop staring.

Then late one night,
toward the end of the summer,
he appeared in my room.
Perhaps that's why
I've always considered him
an angel: silent, innocent, pale
even in the dark.
He undressed
and pulled back the sheet,
slid next to me.
His fingers felt for my lips.

But perhaps I am not remembering
correctly.
Perhaps he never came
into my room that night.
Perhaps he never existed
and I invented him.

Or perhaps it was me, not blond
but dark, who sat all summer
on that sunny corner: seventeen
and struggling to outlast
my own restlessness.

—David Trinidad

MISDEMEANOR

Driving down 54th St at 3 am, we were
Thieves stealing the orange of the street
lamps and the empty coffee cups
littering the sidewalk.
You leaned over, smelling of mint
lip-gloss, and kissed my neck.

And I didn't have to check, to see
if anyone was watching, because they weren't;
the streets were empty. And I kissed you back,
for the first time, under the traffic light.
Exchanging breath and a pulse, I lost myself
in your hair, the line of your collarbone,
inhaling the smell that steamed from your skin.

And we stayed that way even after the light turned
green. Because it didn't matter
that you were a girl
and so was I. Because no one was there
to witness the crime.

—Sharon Zetter

Sombreo Beach, Vancouver Island, BC

Clearing the break in the trail, making it all the way from
Point No Point in just a day, I momentarily understand
what this life is about, ironically, during the washout
in high tide when the landscape is obscured and the trail lost.
And so am I, unsure of either direction or life until the tired
and unimposing sun begins to rest behind the peninsula
to the north, where the treeline doubles in the depths.
The layers of stone are tousled upon the shore as the angry
storm of the ocean spends itself by pulling out, lapping,
throwing stone, seaweed, driftwood upon stone,
every subsequent strata, each day, creating new chaos
and violence, the aftermath of motion and loving fiercely.
                              My bare feet ache
as I gather stone that stack to form the uneven
walls of the fire ring. Naturally, this is where I think
of loving you, the only place that seems right, a refuge
composed of rocks and hard places on this body
of land inextricably caught between old growth and ocean.
                              You love me barefoot
which means loving the knots of my ankles, my feet, themselves—
those two shameful and retarded children let out to play naked
only here, and my twisted toes, contorted and crippled roots of
flesh burrowing into the shore.
                         You come
to me from the ocean like a mermaid who has grown
legs and is walking for the first time. You offer stone totems . . .
a fish, deer, hummingbird. I return: mountain lion,
sea-turtle, six-toed bear. The evening stars offer a distorted
copy of themselves in the shimmering waves
crashing to shore in a collusion of celestial bodies, your
body, my body, changing from mammal to reptile to bird again

and again, my action your reaction, my breathing
becomes your fish-woman breath as entwined mermaid legs
and old chewed-on roots fig snugly around each other
and fuse with salt and earth—two spoons scooping sand,
one continuously overflowing and filling the hollow of the other.
                                    Just past the horizon,
concealed by the darkness, is the invisible line in the ocean
and the distance recedes into America, *our* soil. And you—
somewhere in Kansas, perhaps. I can almost believe
there is terra firma there, beyond the vastness,
on the other side of the Juan de Fuca Straight.

—Carrie Boden

I Think You Got Me Confused

You musta' got me switched
With another hand
I don't answer to Queer
Or Faggot man
Don't need Will and Grace
To get me through the week
No Pride or rainbow stickers
OR GLBT "community" I think

I speak high school rodeo
Compete in FFA
My straight friends ain't breeders
Though we know I'm gay
Dipping my Skoal
Driving Beat up trucks
I like wide-open spaces
And dream of trying my luck

I don't do disco
I sing Garth Brooks
I like Wrangler Jeans
I ride a Quarter Horse.
I fight for a place called here
Just staying small town put
Looking for likewise
This big sky place for us.
I think for myself
Make my own way
Only part of my politics
Speaks that I am gay.
I still eat meat

Two-step on Fridays
Church on Sunday
Praying a cowboy comes my way

I wonder if you're looking too
Somewhere's out there
Just trying your luck
Hoping your life moves on
While staying put
Under wide open spaces
Ropin' Riding, and wreckin'
Praying we find our place.

Not all boys speak city
Not all youth move
Not all of communities hate us
Some lives flow smooth
I think you ain't seen nothing
Of small town life
I think there's more
Than one queer truth

—Timothy Anderson

AWAKENING

I lie in bed
listening to my breath
      his breath, breath

I am fully clothed
and sweat beads on my face
      his face, face

I begin to be lost in the heat
I pull the cover over my body
      his body, body

I dreamt I slept beside myself
consumed by my heat
      his heat, heat, heat

—John G. de la Parra, Jr.

HERE'S A MATCH . . .

To burn the bridge
Between your pussy
And your brain.

Maybe you don't have to
Choose which team to bat for,
And maybe you don't have to
Climb down that fence.

And my, my,
Isn't straddling fun?
We can find a room
Shaped like a circle

(Yes, we can paint it pink)

To make it easier on you,
Because a round one
Won't have corners
We can wedge our hearts
To crouch and cry in.

The world can fall down
On you, and we can
Drink you dry

While trying to find out
How many licks it takes
To get to your center.

Trepidation can be replaced
With rug burns as hazards of
Occupation

And just so we secure
A place in heaven,
Teach me solace tonight
So we can pray to every God
That has a name,
To make sure
We've got all bases covered.

—Krissi Banzon

UNTITLED

an excerpt from the novel *volant*

first thought in my head waking up was, oh no.

i can't say.

it was that girl.

lee.

and

and

a wondering.

veins of her hands generous. thriving.

healthy dirt under her nails.

is she awake now?

and my mom's early morning voice pulling at me.

be Normal, says the tone of her voice.

breakfast is ready.

everything is Fine.

there is a disturbing hum alive in my body. i can hear it over
mom's footsteps.

that brooklyn hum of no source.

it gets into my bones

throws my heart out of whack.

(the earth vibrates with a specific resonance.

a hum, they say.

you can measure its amplitude in the trees, they say.)

there aren't enough trees in brooklyn.

there are: generators, garbage trucks, air conditioners, satellite tvs,
switch buildings. neighbors with machinery, always constructing
things. there are helicopters. airplanes.

and

and there are girls.

* * * *

lee swoops in on me from elsewhere.
makes me lay my head down on my desk.
what did lee say?
that she always knew she liked girls. was sure of it from third
grade:
transfixed by anna shay's smile
transfixed by the monday tuesday wednesday underwear rumpled
up above the waistband
by her toughskins
her soft skin

* * * *

i think i forgot. i've forgotten so much.
the night i woke up hot under too many afghans. my True Best
Friend's leg thrown over my hips.
mouth silent.
fast breath.
i breathe once, she breathes three times.
yes, i remember counting. cataloguing the numbers.
one two three breaths. she.
oh man, *she*.
she mumbled in her sleep.
i remember.
nonsense alien talk.
"oh really," i say. "tell me more."
her hot leg shifts.
hot under afghans, chill air in the winter room and i lay there and
can't sleep.

she

says to a bathroom fulla girls, "yeah i got it on with jamie bickford,"
conspires in my ear "no way. no way a boy's getting down my pants
just yet."
the fire. god i didn't know what it was then.
the fire in me from how she said *pants*.

i wake up that night,
her wrestler leg thrown across me
skyblue toenails poking through the afghan holes.
i count her breath, like sheep.

—robin pickering

SONG TO MYSELF AT SEVENTEEN

I didn't know how to save you then,
so forgive me. How you were able
to latch onto your spirit and go on
breathing, astonishes me even now.
Even though you knew who wrote
Faggot on your locker in indelible ink
your junior year, you never said a word.
And still somehow, you kept going.
In your mind, you sang to them
and your voice filled them with light.
You imagined they became your friends:
the ones who stole your gym bag,
smashed the headlights on your car,
or yelled Queer down the hall at you.
Still, you kept walking. And singing.
Quietly, almost silently, to yourself.
But then, how you found the courage
to take on the choir solo, I'll never know.
Your lips trembled next to the mic.
At first, a tremor, catch in the throat.
Then the first notes, unsteady
and broken, but poised to soar.
Flaming Caruso. How you torched
the auditorium with your song.
Then afterwards, the handshakes
and back pats from the prom king,
captain of the varsity football team.
All docile. All dumbstruck. All yours.
Until you left alone that night.
I didn't know then. If I could have
somehow stood next to you,

walked you to your car. Made sure
you got safely through the dark parking lot.
Now some twenty years later,
I still touch my throat. That thin line
of raised white scar tissue. But
I am not silent. I'm singing
to the you who once was me,
and to all the brave Carusos
who dream their voices into the world,
a little wounded, but on fire.

—Gerard Wozek

BUTTERFLYING

queerness is an art form

one moment we are who we seem to be
a sushi chef
a costume designer
a racecar driver
and then we re-invent ourselves
we become
flame throwers
go go dancers
organic gardeners

the transformations are more beautiful every time

we are silver-winged butterflies

butterflies are fashion bugs
trampoline beings
trans-porters
trans-genic
trans-gressive
trans-everything

butterflies are us

queerness is an art form.

one moment we are who we seem to be
a dreamer
a drummer
a mathematician

and then we do the butterfly

we become another invention of ourselves

we become the woman on the moon
the man who spins around the room
the flying flower children
punk philosophers
computer hackers
cyber sluts
queer ones
hard ones
perfumed ones

we become all this
and more
we become all we want
queens
saints
sinners
swimmers
becoming ourselves
transforming
transfiguring
transcending
transgendering
trans-everything
butterflying

—Tatiana de la Tierra

LAS BARBIES

Was it her eyes?
Her smell
Smile
Laugh

That have me all locota
Crazy

Thinking about her
My friend

We played Barbies together
Some we picked up at a yard sale

No matter
It was a toy

A Barbie
With a fancy sock as a tube dress
And we took turns brushing her hair
And you talked about the boys
And I listened to your experienced creativity
Your serious wonder

I was angry that I couldn't have you talk that way about me
Share those thoughts about me

Have my Barbie with a Mexican accent kiss your blue eyed doll
Mine with dirty brown hair
And yours playing the role of the teacher-kiss mine
Because we couldn't afford a Ken

—Madeline Alviso

MAMA SAID

I was so involved with boy-rhythms that I never came to grips with the
fact that I was a girl. I was twelve years old when my mother took me
inside and said, "You can't be wrestling outside without a T-shirt on." It
was a trauma. —Patti Smith

Mama said I was a girl,
to stop that curl in my lip—
get off my boy trip
stop tearing off my shirt with the wrestlers
pretty soon my tits would get big.

Mama said I was a girl so stop naming my vagina
my bologna sandwich, my deli ham, my easy cheese
ate over easy die sleazy I'm easy squeezing
into a tight black skirt I squirt
I sliced it on the side to make getting it on easier.

Mama said I was a girl,
but I fuck like hamburger
finding myself the queen of erotic fast love.

Mama said I was a girl,
and I built buildings out of fear
prayed to god I'd end up queer.

Mama said,
Mama said,
Mama said I was a girl,
and I pretended to die.

—Andrea Shipley

HIDE-N-SEEK

I am greeted by a hand holding straws
then a voice, *pull and see if you're it.*

He and I have the same size straws
so we hide with each other

under a barbed wire fence
to the edge of the pasture

freshly plowed by a tractor—
tires big as rolls of hay—

behind which we hide.
In a sudden fever of attachment,

we find each other—
he unbuckles my belt

then pushes my pants
past my knees knocking each other—

despite the stories of Sodom,
of disease, despite Grandpa calling me an 'ole sissy.

—Scott Bailey

WE ARE NOT VEGETARIANS

We are not Vegetarians—
We like what we do
And we do.

—Miek Coccia

CLOCK

attraction comes from the mind
me, I want to touch him. bad
I want to know everything
still is going to be alright,
hope for him,
so I follow him around
look at the floor,
follow his lead.
He is searching books
in the back of the antique store,
the dust covers shelve us in.
me behind him,
He faces me forward
I want to touch
black his jacket
his hair smell
nuzzle against his neck.
I want to get inside of him,
and I want to fall forward.
I want him inside me, beside me,
In front of me
I see his nape, the back of his neck,
I want to fall forward, to trace
my prints there, to grasp him
with this clutch wrapped around him,
gentle, and pull him near, as
He almost backs up into me, and
We meet, but he turns, pouting now
because his shoe is untied.

He's twice my years, and
I want to hold him like I would a child
I bend down and tie a knot for him,
I could so easily be gone
then had a clock to punch,
when he asked now what

—Douglas A. Martin

THE LOGIC OF QUEERNESS:
(RELEASING YOUR IVY EVENING WITHIN)

Evening will find itself in me. —James Joyce (*Ulysses*)

A feeling like the onset of an evening: pregnant with growling thunder
will find itself growing inside you. Yes it will begin with a growling
inside your body.
After the thunder calms and jells: gathering sound into a fluttering
green angelfish,
It will begin to move slow-motion with translucent wings
And you will feel an underwater waving trigger a transformation
(Yes, it will happen inside your body) awakening your fleeing
desire.

It will happen in your bed, it will happen in the mall,
It will happen watching television, it will happen
In front of your computer, it will happen
At the dinner table, it will happen in Math class, It will happen
In the car at a stop light as you sit with your mother waiting for
your life to change.

And yes, you will say nothing: no, you will not say one word about
it to anyone.

The fluttering green angelfish will begin dropping
Snippets of desire like tiny green seeds
Between the glass walls of your mind—floating angelically
Like a hand made of green jelly—numbing your consciousness
With a python's pointed precision.

The logic of queerness never involves fairness. Shame:wounded
Until one of those bright green seeds
Appears one day in your mouth
while you are brushing your teeth,
Sticking out your tongue
while you are standing naked
In front of your bathroom mirror,
yes, you will be frozen with fear.
You will look at yourself directly in your eyes
and say, no, absolutely not,
And again your body will go
Frozen with fear.   Go further.
You will survive on your own planning.

This newly found seed strange and slick will grow like and invisible ivy—it will grow from your mouth—invisible to all except
those who have a twin seed hidden under their own terrified
tongues.

The invisible ivy will slowly creep over your ears, wind its way
around your fears and slowly wrap around your throat. Perhaps
you will want to give in
and allow the ivy to sap your strength
and strangle you, yes, perhaps you will
let your self be choked by what the seed has made.
Or perhaps you will want to sing,
make a song of the seed,
yes, seek out the others
who are surely singing the same quiet song.

Your silence will not protect you, Audre Lorde wrote, and this I
learned to be true:
Your silence will depend on you. It will also depend on what

country, what city,
What town you live in. It will depend on the laws that have been
made and re-made to make you Fear your desire, or worse, laws
that have been made to prevent you
From ever finding your match, your partner, your love who makes
you giddy
With life, the one you found with the bright green seed hiding
under the tongue.

Perhaps you will want to burn down your desire with your vol-
canic rage: a rage
That has swelled like a giant translucent lava wave
Inside you with each joke that you hear about boys who like boys.
Or girls who like girls. Or boys who act like feminine girls or girls
Who act like masculine boys or someone who's just different from
anyone
In your family. And the town,
Someone who wears all black or all pink or all brown.
Or someone almost exactly like you who's just not sure yet
Who will be the one to love you.
Perhaps you will want to shave your desire down
With your shame; perhaps you will want your desire to drown
in its own fear of singing.

It will swim its way back to the back of your throat, it will grow
back double
And make a mental moat around your consciousness, trapping
desire
Within your force-field like a lonesome queen waving a pink silk
scarf
From the stone tower of your mind.

Perhaps you will not want to free the seed to grow
Where it wants to grow, perhaps you will
Want no one to know of your seed's need to grow. Instead you will
Construct a permanent smile made from your own hiding; per-
haps you will
Try to burn back the ivy that keeps growing from that original
seed of desire.
But you will want to survive. I will tell you how I survived.

Finally, after years of hating myself even though I was a star foot-
ball player. After years Of hating myself, even though I won
medals in track. After years
Of hating myself, even though I made high honors in high school.
After years
Of hating myself, even though I was king of my prom. After years
Of hating myself, even though I had friends and family who loved
me:
I almost ran out of breath as the invisible ivy was getting tighter
and tighter like a tether
Of sad snow around my neck.   Finally,
I let all the seeds grow, grow, and grow
Until they kept growing and covered me with ivy so strong
And vibrant and unique that it became my reason for living.
The seed that began inside me finally taught me to sing.
It became a source of love and beauty instead of my reason
For wanting to disappear from the planet.
The black evening contains a wild field of sky: coded with ancient
instruction.
The same sky will follow you for your entire life: use the scattered
and stunning stars
as a map to survive!

—Ron Palmer

This I Whisper

Young man with desires so bad, he needs to save the world
To prove he might be somewhat good.

Mom and Dad don't touch him; he must be broken.
Stars do not answer him, God won't talk to him,
Leaves of grass keep their secrets; he must be a lunatic.
He's a salmon swimming upstream, using his tail to go against

The flow. His tail is a time machine, taking him back and forth
Toward the source. His Speedo is a wet loincloth
As he names himself Super Kinky-guy, with the power
To perturb the Universe, leap out of closets

Rediscover the Shining Face in the Cosmic Womb
Before conception. This I whisper into queer tender ears:
It's okay, it's okay, to be sensual, to desire, to share your tale of
survival.
We save the world just by swimming in it.

—Horehound Stillpoint

THE ODD YEARS
after Robin Carr

Age 3: I cry in tub as mob of older brother and sisters wearing
cheap Halloween masks come into bathroom, jump up and down,
scream, and flick light on and off

Age 5: I wear fake Ray-Ban's to Kindergarten and tell Mrs.
Goodwin I have terrible eye disease. She's concerned, calls home,
then confiscates sunglasses.

Age 7: I decide to take up hairdressing and give my dog a haircut.
Sister sees my "creation", says mom will kill me. I hide in garage
and use Elmer's Glue to re-attach Sugarfoot's hair.

Age 9: I am shunned by the other Indians at an Indian Guides
campout for having long hair and am told I look llike a girl. I win
friends by eating chocolate marshmallow cookies in Dad's new
bright yellow Mercury Capri and inviting curious tribe members
in to stick parts out of sunroof.

Age 11: I throw a pool birthday for myself and invite eleven boys
from school. I dance naked on diving board, singing along with
my favorite 45: "baby we can do it, take your time, do it right, we
can do it ba-by, do it tonight."

Age 13: I discover ejaculation while sliding down the rope in gym
class. I linger after bell rings, climb up and slide down five times
before Mr. Smith blows his whistle and screams, "Conway, you'll
injure your 'pulotus'!"

He's like the many moons of Jupiter
and bubbles that burst
about the heads of children
It's a powerful little body that he carries
like a tight little fistful of gumballs
The envy of other little boys nearby
—among them me!
We all long to fill our mouths with the multi-colored
kid-like chaotic marbles of chewing,
precious and highly prized
for the slippery sweetness
they'll set free upon our tongue

His little booted feet have kicked me
His knobby knees elbow my sides
that split with laughter
and I roll onto the floor
A little sowbug
in sweetest danger

He's the boy rolling fast
a giant tire down a road
bouncing with rubbery glee

We're two balls bouncing
loosed from the playground
by wild kicking children
and ricocheting
through traffic
and parking meters
and over the heads of pedestrians
through tunnels
and precariously over suspension bridges

Up over hedges
and down harrowing alleyways
past red and yellowbright signs
that with frustration
seek to guide us on our laughing, sprung path

That big yellow ball
that falls down finally each day
and the moon that rolls on through behind it
lay us low in time
We come upon an empty field
our bouncing and our ricocheting spent
and finally winding to a sputter
long to rest the one against the other

And after the cool giggling evening of crickets
and all things that jump and sing
What must it be like to lay as river stones with him
under a thousand stars
that make the water
shimmer above us
like his smile?

—Trebor Healey

LONGING

It wasn't just about sex, but about
watching Miss America and having
your heart broken by the wrong beauty,

about no longer being worried about
your hands waving about, about tight
pants as a uniform for a secret war.

My father told my mother that I was
forbidden to learn how to iron or cook.
I can still change tires, wear a tool belt

as if a figleaf. Do you have a girlfriend?
asked drunk relatives. No. Anything more
would be dangerous: no. Theater was

stolen from me, feminine space, and so
I never auditioned. I was allowed to worship
astronauts, men who showered with

each other, men who left the Earth and then
ached for it. A gaze was a fire escape
from the blindness around me. Gazes were

an education far from schools where boys
gave me black eyes because they had blue balls.
Don't act like such an adult, Father said often.

He didn't know that my homeroom was more
room than home, that I was a threat not yet
sure of my powers, that when Miss America

got crowned, that I wept too for her, us,
that we were visible and perfect at last.
Tears, sweat and semen seemed linked

but I almost failed my science classes.
I wanted Alchemy 101. I wanted reasons
why I couldn't be as naked as Adam or atoms.

—Rane Arroyo

FORT

atop the fences where the four yards met
started god knows how long ago
from demos, renos, a ceiling Doug Laird
said smelled like a dog house—a fort
from which a car antennae doubled as a flagpole
(though a flag was never agreed upon)
it picked up signals from whatever we made up inside
at the time

girls would not go there
not allowed, or they did not want to (I forget)
but we returned to it, years later, to talk, kiss
sometimes more than that. There was
never a line-up: if you went, if it was empty—when you left
there was no one else around

but you were seen, of course, and it was always by someone who
had never been inside
that did all the talking. There was always someone hiding
in the bushes.One of them, I remember, became a reporter.
Quite famous. Broke a story on child pornography
"and was lured," as she put it,

to Los Angeles, where she worked in television and became old
like the rest of us. When she retired her network did a special on
her. She told the story of a fort she built with another kid (me),
how she was a tomboy and I was "probably gay"—and "isn't it
funny
how we keep returning to these things, years later,
after leaving them so long," our roles
irretrievably reversed

—Michael Turner

47

After School Commute with My Girl*

"Are you feeling better now?" "I'll be fine." "You're such a sweet heart, you know that Janine?" "You too." "Don't let those whores at school get you down." "I figure they'll be hosing down our Lexus anyway, why bother?"

i'm gonna tell you something good its like those chicks with the catholic school skirts all plaid and booty cuttin' yeah boy and they got the legs going down to there in them tight ass knees socks and oh snap they about to kiss now oh my god this is better than pay per view dog so much better than all that oh my gawd they can't be more than sixteen and seventeen yo man check it out now

"If I ask really nicely, maybe my brother could be our donor." "Cool! Your brother rocks." "Yeah, I know." "Unless you want to adopt." "Whichever one." "Do you want a boy or a girl?" "Anything, as long as it's happy."

that is just the most disgusting thing, little black girl and a little white girl on the train acting like they was married i hope my daughters never do anything like that, isn't that right my god those people make me sick to my stomach them homosexuals what do they think this is a peep show keep it in the bedroom

"Which one... Canada or Vermont?" "Angela..." "Janine...answer me. Honestly." "Vermont." "Or Europe." "Amsterdam would be so fun." "Not too much fun." "Hey!"

i can't believe its them I knew they were best friends but this is ridiculous that's what they were doing the time we couldn't find them and they were late for class jesus save the pda for some-where else that is so obnoxious wait till i tell everybody you guys are done they can't even see me from this side of the car they'll never know

"Can I call you tonight?" "No, it'll look too suspicious." "All right, I'll see you tomorrow." "Sure, I'll walk with you a bit, I have to switch cars anyway." "Why?" "Cause I'm sick of the people in this car." "I love you so much." "I love you, too."

—L. B.

*The words that are not in italics are taken almost verbatim from people who think that we can't hear what they're saying.

SALTBOX BROTHEL

I was a body. I was a laboratory. I was okay with that.
We used my house, we climbed the back stairs, we told
my mother we were *meditating*. She was psychic,
but her old plaid nightgown like a cocktail dress
and the little straw sweating over the glass—
I wouldn't mention her Bailey's and she
wouldn't mention my looks.

On the happiest day of my life. On Presidents' Day.
Upstairs, a good citizen, my dress was big and my bed even bigger.
Three kids came to see me. We took turns on the mattress.
I said *be quiet* at regular intervals. Someone said
what next? Someone suggested we use a coin.

Crossed my legs, made my pretty face, listened
for my father's car. He was head-on. He'd be
home soon, but I didn't say so. Watched a blonde head
on a brown one. Watched my own hand go down. At some point
it occurred to me, this was going to be fun.

—Danielle Pafunda

SUNSHINE

i awoke with the yellow bright morning

helping me store your

hands gliding underneath my clothes,

lips warm with longing and bitten in desire,

fingers searching for my being,

breasts supple in ecstasy,

and eyes reflecting paradise,

in my chest and—

lending a hand

to throw away boxes of

weathered pasts.

clouds were nowhere in sight

birds chirped

and rainbow smiled.

no more rain.

—Macel Aguilar

A TEXAS SUNRISE

The light goes out.
Darkness floods the room.
Small breeze enters through an open window,
Solemnly shattering silence.

Laughter shoots through the darkness like a laser.
Male voice utters simple sarcasms.
Insecurity dissolves into comfort.
Barriers drown in sweet perfume.

Click.
Fluorescence magnifies beauty.
Romance illuminated by soft purple glows.
Voice laughs at stereotypical situation.

Eyes roll amusingly.
Silver strings of affection grow taut.
Two beings clinging to one another
In sweet innocence.

Bodies not betraying,
Desire not pushing,
Simple satisfaction.
Separate sinews coexisting in pure ecstasy.

Lips press.
Arms hold.
Beauty manifested in vulnerability.
Strength created in joined weaknesses.

Sun rises.
Dawn breaks.
Molten light brews in an outdoor cauldron,
Bubbles over the windowpane.

Flame consumes shadows,
Casting them aside.
Blinding ignorance destroys
What only the night can understand.

Intolerant daylight curses nocturnal magnificence.
Warm contentment drowns in harsh judgment.
But memory, emotion, experience
Endure.

How does Condemnation justify itself?
In all its stupid splendor?
Beauty interpreted as appalling,
Suffering accepted.

Night allows the Day to maintain its ignorant arrogance.
Aware of her own cosmic fabulosity,
Confident in her own capacity,
Her dance knows no bounds.

—Jay Brannan

EARPLUGS

Putty globes
thumbs press
into place;

drifting to sleep
beside him
for the first time,

trying to: his
seemingly distant
muffled snore

more than heard
—felt, at intervals;
and in between:

interior sound
of my breathing,
my heart.

—Francisco Aragón

BLACK WATER CREEK

Remember how you tried to wash it
from your skin and his—
the red clay spinning down the drain,

its swirls of tainted yellow
clinging to you
as you both bathed that day, naked

in the slow ripples of the creek,
he and you, clothes on the bank
damp and daring.

How seeing the slick line
of his waist, its dashed
newness, white warmth under

so much dirt, in the sun as
you both lay, determined to see
underneath, that which you'd followed

in cloth and denim or the scuffed
rim of a shoe. How you taunted him,
begged him to come

in the house
where you tracked those
muddy stains, stripped down

to the steamy mirror
where he bolted wet from his pants again
stepped into the rushing stream,

how you didn't know what
else you wanted, watching
his form, wanting

only to delay his going,
standing as you both
were unprepared—that sad hour when the sun

moved in and behind the clouds
and the green birch trees and
long-drooping vines hung

where the woods were lanky and
white, the soil-red
surface flowing

below, his body a thing
forbidden, no way
to dive in, just wade.

No way to slip him around you
the sliding white
of the towel, a slow glide.

—Walter R. Holland

MARIPOSA

In Mexico
There's not a Spanish word for Gay
People say
Mariposa   Butterfly
To mock our "batting eyelids"
To say we're weak   Maybe flighty   Maybe dumb as air
But if you think about it

Mariposa is not much of an insult after all
The most vulnerable creature in the world
The caterpillar
Is the ultimate survivor
Cheating death with every inch
Moving patiently inside its burden of a coat
Exposed   All neck and hair

But when it springs out of its dark cocoon
Who wouldn't want to be compared
With such a burst of freedom
Mariposa milagrosa
Applause of color
Champion
Miracle extraordinaire

—Rigoberto González

Last Ditch

The one day of my life I had a girlfriend
was the first time someone asked me point blank
if I was gay. I was happy, thought Jennifer could end
something vague I was heading for. Trent tanked
that theory. Trent was curious and joking. I think
I could even have said yes, but I didn't want *fag* inked
into my life yet. There would have been therapy,
problems—I was fourteen and at a school with Christian enmity
between the fundamentalists, Catholics and Mormons.
The person to feel bad for in this poem is Jennifer.
I never saw her after the awkward moment I asked her
out. It was the last day of the eighth grade. She'd written
that she loved me in my yearbook. I thought I had to
ask her out. Jennifer, I'm sorry. It wasn't you.

—Jason Schneiderman

ARRYTHMIA (1–10)

1. I know that none of this goes anywhere.

2. At school there's a new boy. He's assigned the desk next to mine and while I'm getting my books for English class he watches me from the corner of his eye and I can sense a kiss coming in the way he recklessly untucks his shirt; drawing my attention to the fact that a number of the buttons are undone giving hints of his solid chest. His name is Peter.

3. He chases me down like a pack of wolves and snaps at me with all his teeth and all his mouths and opens me with all his claws and lays his panting tongues on my heart and laps up all the sweet yearning with which it is filled until I am empty and groaning.

4. When I'm home from school and even Peter's body is not enough to distract me I have to deal with the fact that my father is a charcoal beast of embers. His fist leaves depressions of ash. My mother is unstitched at the seams; at the joins of her shoulders you can peer in and see darkness and stars. I come from that darkness and back to that darkness I will go.

5. Peter takes me to the old cemetery to hold my hand and when we kiss I can feel all these ghosts wanting to be alive again.

6. I go to his house and climb into his bed and take him in my hands and make him cum like thunder and he makes so much noise I worry his mother will hear.

7. He comes to my place of exile and we talk about Star Wars movies and he stays the long night and we jerk each other off and afterwards when we're hugging I say 'This feels completely natu-

ral' and he says 'I know . . . it feels right'. I don't say so but it's the first time I've ever felt really 'at home' with someone else. I can't remember why we stop seeing each other.

8. After that he is always trying to sit next to me, to get my attention. He is like a hummingbird. My lips a succulent flower. Sometimes I take mercy on him and send him a withering smile.

9. I write him a note that says:

What you hear when I speak is the blood curdling yorp of animals in the abattoir; the terrified pant of a gazelle in the tiger's mouth; the scream of mothers in places where children grow into graves the way they should grow into hand-me-down clothes. What you hear when I speak is the burning up of life.

10. He stays away.

—Dallas Angguish (written when the poet was fifteen)

THE BOY GIRL GAME

I'm a boy with my cousin
she's the only one
who lets me do this

We play in her room
use pillows to kiss
kissing is like this with us;
(*would it be so bad*
without pillows)
I want to find out

I wear Jim Morrison t-shirts
spend my allowance on baseball cards
and wish every night

that when I wake
I'll be looking down at a boy's body
instead of mine

which reminds me of how
I hate morning
when I can see myself;

how I like the dark
where I don't have to be she
when I pray
to whoever it is
twelve year olds pray to
that when I wake I'll wake as a boy

—Jody Helfand

POLESTAR

Your dream (you tell me
    late at night, your voice
a Sunday whisper so
    your mother cannot hear
her son has called *that* boy

again): to lie naked
    in a field looking
at star-choked sky.
    I nod and picture
a small bright zigzag

hanging high above
    the horizon. *That's*
Cassiopeia the faithless
    queen who gave her child
to the sea I'd tell you

and this is the Big Dipper.
    Follow those low stars
to find due North. Now
    I understand I long
to show you a thing

I've never found alone
    but this much I know:
Where I am? *Beside you*
    on the grass, in the field
next to the dam, guiding

your eyes to some far-off
    spark. Where are you?
Seeking strange constellations.
    I can't speak; you orbit
like those mythic glimmers
overhead: elusive, remote.

—Christopher Stahl

HEAT.

Day 1

Bead of sweat
Gathers at the peak of an
Inner thigh precipice—
Slides—uncertain—then
Plunges,
Clinging to the clammy surface,
Down to unprobed depths
Below.

It begins Thus.

Day 2

I awake with a gasp.

A sudden heat wave has sent tingling tremors
upwards and outwards from a throbbing source,
as yet unchartered.

I do not like the unfamiliar, tepid cling of
sweaty pyjamas.

Day 3

And it won't go away.

According to my gran's electrothermomemeter
the temperature under my tongue—
in the crook of my armpit—

and even in the crease of my bum hole
is NORMAL.
(Note: I want to find the person who says these bits are best for
proper temperature reading
and see how they like it).

It must be wrong.

Day 4

Physics is my Savior.
Everything in the Universe makes sense and
even has a mathematical equation for the
non-believers.
So
if whatever is sending my blood
racing through its tunnels at double-speed,
is not generating any additional thermal energy
then—

Then I am possessed by a wily fire demon.
Then I am officially a freak of nature.

Day 5

Alas!
That this wretchèd waif may be
Destin'd to roam the kingdom,
Engulf'd by the swoonsome flush of a
Lusty flame, which
Burns betwixt nape and kneecap!

Day 6

A sweltering haze bounces off
Car bumpers and overflowing dustbins.
As I walk down the empty high street
two men cross the road towards me.
I feel trapped.
Frantically, my eyes dart away as the
monster inside me leaps up
like a dog—crazy with feverish recognition—
straining to be reunited with Master.

A bitch in heat?

Day 7

And the veil of childhood—
already hanging by a loose thread,
falls away to reveal Truth.

This unrelenting urge to
scratch—this—unreachable itch—this
inexpressible yearning is
Why the men I see, chase women and
Why the women I see, allow themselves to be caught.
Why doors are locked and screams are muffled and
all mornings are heavy with silence.
Why several girls around the way
fall at the first hurdle and still
hurl themselves at two or three more,
their glow fading before their
adolescence is even over.
Why it is so easy to fall.

The 'one thing' that always leads to 'another'.

This cursèd heat is what makes
The world go round.
The world in which I am merely another
Heat-driven, heat-seeking hormone missile—a
Time-bomb, fuelled by the
Combustion that turns a
Bright spark into a
Womanly flame.

Thus
on the Seventh Day
this not-so-secret mystery is revealed to me—
and I panic.

—Onika Simon

MY SIXTH GRADE SEX LIFE:
MILNE ELEMENTARY, NEW ORLEANS

Up and down the wide wooden stairways
of that musty, spinsterish school building
I contrived always to lag behind the others

chubby, clumsy, easily ashamed, the butt
of every fag joke. I had a girlfriend,
Suzannah, the D.A.'s daughter, precocious,

devout. Weekends, we made our sanctuary
among trees at a nursery, where we kissed
between lovers' talk about death and sin.

In class, boys passed sketches of tits—mine
drew laughs, a pointy pair of witches' hats.
But I was smart, polite—teachers loved me,

boys didn't trust me, girls thought I was nice.
Walking back from church together, Suzannah
and I held hands, a small embrace that felt wholly

adult, although later, sprawled on my bedroom floor
with my best friend John, listening to Kiss
and looking at wrestling mags, I wanted

to see John naked, especially his ass,
and I didn't know why. Was it John who told me
about Scott getting caught with another kid

"doing a double blowjob"? Up and down
the stairs I stumbled, trying to get it straight.
Blowing what? up? down? out? A swollen maze

of tubes, every picture my mind designed
looked stranger than any truth. Finally,
I asked. "You know," John smirked, knowing I didn't:

"sixty-nine." Patient pornographer, he detailed
the mechanics of the act. Why would Scott
want to do that, I wondered, wishing Scott

or John would show and tell me, praying sex
might happen without a thought, without touch,
like grace, Suzannah saying, "Sinners die."

—Brad Richard

Soft

Soft
Soft breath
soft touches
soft emotions

There can be no sin
in this tender, throbbing passion
pulsing through me.

In this euphoria
of senses and skin
resulting from a simple caress

Inn the gently indulgent embrace
of two women mingling,
limbs and sheets entwined in sacred prayer

There is no sin
in this, this profound
expressive tenderness,

soft elation
soft desire
soft love
soft

—Jennifer L. Shakan

MICKEY MOUSE

Everyone knows it was swampland.
Useless, 'gator patrolled muck-juice.
Acre upon acre of it, like primeval

vaudeville. Ridiculous growth, antic
life. Along came Walt. He raised his roll
of blueprints like a wand and,

Shazaam! Everybody knows the rest.
My dad took us kids down there once.
It was all right. Dad was acting rich again,

so we got the grand tour. The lady,
I forget her name, smiled and explained
the maze of underground passages

beneath it all: Goofy carrying his head
and loping through to lunch. I liked
the *Haunted Mansion* and *Mr. Toad's*

Wild Ride. I don't know though. At twelve
or thirteen, a boy's body is already
a pretty wild ride. Dad's enthusiasm

was a little nerve-wracking. The whole place,
really. The word *relentless* comes to mind.
Don't get me wrong, I'm not one of those post-

suburban sourpusses, knocking Spielberg
and Ronald McDonald all the time. Well,
maybe I am. I remember when Dad caught

me masturbating. *Mortifying.*
I endured a forty-minute lecture on hormones
and cleanliness. As if being *tidy* would protect

me from messes like syphilis or homosexuality.
Fact is, no one can keep all the muddy stuff out.
Anyone with any sense knows that.

—Christopher Murray

SOMETHING MORE OBVIOUS

We loved our bodies nine years old,
lean and hairless, not yet shaped,
as if anything could happen.
I wish we could be boys, you said
lying next to me in your grandmother's bed,
our dreams spelled out on the ceiling.
We could wear tube socks
and play baseball, hard
not soft, overhand with sliding.

In the backyard
we built a clubhouse out of scrap lumber,
painted it yellow and silver.
That summer it survived the tornado that scattered
the neighbor's garage all over the alley,
and we danced around it
with our hammers over our heads.

Later it would be the boyish girls
who would haunt us, the drive-thru girl
at Dairy Queen with her shaved head,
still too beautiful to be a boy.
At the high school dance our eyes would meet,
but we would be too shy for each other,
we would turn our eyes toward the ceiling.

Our dream interrupted
by something more obvious, bulging
out of a tight pair of Levi's.
And we quietly danced against it
with our imaginary hammers over our heads,
our arms growing weaker, our bodies
growing softer, now knowing what to love.

—Amanda R. Evans

WOLF PACKET AND RURAL AMERICA

pull out the tractor and rev her up
the mice are chewing on rubber tires
the pitchforks are poked into the hay
next to the book of poems by d.a.levy
acker is undone
while the grain is shipped to Arizona
she is booked
in queer
grammar
Alaska received the greens so
lay down your guns
and spin
it's time to undo your ears
littering your pinna in nervous response
take off your flannel and hang it on the branch
rural America is all punked out
speak up lisp
fearless
tougher than you think
middle American unions
mommy's partner
hi Christina

—Matthew Wascovich

Spending the Night

Now, in another part of the country,
I hear it called "staying over."
Back then, a couple of years
was a gaping difference
The ornately carved door
covering the strings of an upright
melded into the headboard
of the bed. He asked
if I had found my way yet
to lending my hand to another guy.
At first, it wasn't clear to me
what he was asking for.
I was barely in my teens,
naïve and proud. He
was breathtaking,
stretched out in the dark,
at ease in his white cotton briefs;
his elbows akimbo, his fingers
interlacing behind his head;
handsome and merciful.
And though he never pressed
his lips to my lips,
he did not find any need
to rebuff my clumsy fingers.

—Scott Hightower

NIGHTFIRE

On the fourth of July
I find myself in the crowds by the river,
lining the bridges for the show.
I've walked here with him,
this new friend who remembers
my name, or what I ate for lunch
and how much I like
Joni Mitchell.
We watch the explosions of sound,
and then, the color;
sea anemones raining down
golden tendrils,
soft against smoke,
haze on hue
and clinging to the cityscape like dust.
I find myself like a child again,
more taken with this feeling
of innocence
than the night-fire,
bewildered that at twenty-two
I can still 'ooh' and 'ahh'.

That night I look at him
and realize this can happen
twice;
my heart knows color.
What I stored away so
deeply, so silently,
a private beauty
pushed up, illuminated by
the colors of the sky

and the way his face
looked in that amber light
I realize I could trade
all the brilliance of that evening
for just one more chance
to be a part of someone else,
a soul shouting,
this one last explosion
cupped and quietly confined
within the word "friend."

—Brad Daugherty

WHEN MY SISTER WAS FIFTEEN

That Thanksgiving my mother made me sit
on the floor. Punishment   for my sister's homosexuality, so obviously my doing: all those
lesbian folk-rock records, those gay boys
I brought home for previous holiday dinners
in high school—Arik, whose parents cast him
aside at sixteen, or Justin, who had his own home
too far away—or the lesbian artists who took me
along for gay pride and community festival, where
I first   registered to vote and reveled in Leah
Delaria's voice beside a boy whose t-shirt showed
Jesse Helms and a rectum side by side and said:
only one of these assholes deserves   your respect.
To think of all the times my mother tried
make me tell her, with promises
she'd love me no matter what; to think
she seemed so fine with my friends and the thought
that I was one of them; to think of her own
friends—open and out and okay in her book. When
my sister's only boyfriend—back in third grade—grew
to be her closest friend in high school and   flaming
all along the way, my mother loved him. When my
roommate and I kissed openly at parties, it was
her my mother couldn't stand. But the year my sister
came out of the closet, I thought: oh, it all makes sense
now, and my mother   thought: Rita must sit on the floor.

—Rita D. Costello

MacArthur High School

Everyday, we step off the bus,
our heavy bags piled on our backs,
walk through the gate,
greeted by his stern brass face,
eternal pipe held firmly in molded lips

The kids who live close by,
in the once-splended neighborhood
behind the athletic field
take the back gate,
avoiding the daily call to action

The ROTC building,
always gleaming
in fresh white paint
squatted there, right
next to the football lawn

You can't get around it

Nerds hang out in the library
I guess that's why
the recruiters always set up there
right across from the desk
where I hand students books

Brochures promise money
education, travel
and above all, computers;
the entire programming class
lines up to hear the call

At home, Sergeant King calls
me every week. We need people like you.
My closet door just creaking open,
I ask about the policy
he laughs, we certainly don't need them

I ask, he tells

Henry wants to join the Coast Guard,
his desert blood longs for salt and wind
they say they'll take him, right after
he crosses the stage, the next day even
until they finally admit, he's too fat

The Army has lower standards,
in their opinion
my dovelike Henry works
with nuclear weapons in Colorado
with only the memory of a sea

Before every football game
we are herded into the courtyard
General MacArthur staring down:
Feo, fuerte, y formal
as the ROTC marches in front of us

Then the bull comes.

Or really, a guy in a suit
stampeding out
as the cheerleaders
drape themselves over him
like the Minotaur's mother

War hangs heavy in the air
with testosterone
we'll kill the enemy
a bunch of other boys
all practicing for the future

We get a speech about honor
about all the strong men
we all certainly know about
whom we, or the football team
will honor on the field tonight

Everyday's a battle at MacArthur High.

—Lacey A. Dalby

MY MYSTERIOUS BODY

I wanted an older brother to show me
existing paths. I had Bruce Springsteen
and Stevie Nicks, ear companeros.

This was before Will and Grace, before
the Hot Chili Peppers waved the American
flag by wearing just tube socks on their

sex on stage, before Queer As Folk became
more soap opera and less blue movie,
before AIDS was seen as God's assassin.

I'd dance alone in my room, music as my
ship out of my birth sign. I wanted to be
anonymous and discovered. I wanted Bruce

to teach me to drive, for Stevie to dress me
for the improbability of my beauty (men
can be beautiful too, gracias Michelangelo).

I was in a maze with a man at the center,
or so I prayed with headphones on. Someone
like me, but not too much, not just a mirror.

—Rane Arroyo

ELEGY FOR THE HURDLER

1971–1989

The track was hot, the lanes were hard and black—
  remember? You didn't even want to run.
Anthony Solomon, if you came back,
  back to the day when we were almost men,

then wouldn't others on the team return,
  somehow, to find a way to keep you off
the track that afternoon, to make you turn,
  turn back? Return—the school will look as if

you hadn't left. Forget the ambulance;
  the asphalt, bloody, burned—you never died.
Come back. Your starting block forbids your stance.
  Your hurdles lowered, stacked, and set aside.

—Randall Mann

GREYHOUND

Sometimes when
I stand

with my ticket
I try

not to catch
the stare of

the unshaven man
in the army

jacket. His
sharp eyes are

lodestones, pulling
my eyes from

a careful
study

of the floor.
He asks me

for a quarter but
my racing heart-

beat and pounding
breath tell him

I know
he could take

so much more.

—Christopher Stahl

THE GIRL IN THE BOY'S DRESSING ROOM

When my grandmother and I shopped for clothes,
we went to the boy's section and looked through
racks of dress shirts and ties, until a salesman
came over and told us where the girl's department was.
I let my grandmother handle this:
Young man, she would say, my granddaughter
feels comfortable wearing boy's clothing.
Will you please help us find her size?
Then, arms filled with clothes, I went to
the boy's dressing room as my grandmother
kept searching for other styles that would fit me.
As she did this, I was aware of the salesman
standing outside my dressing room, switching from
one foot to the other, describing pretty dresses—
trying to take the girl out of the boy's dressing room.

—Jody Helfand

COURAGE!

My Eyes are
Brown!
I know, how do I find it so easy
To Admit
I hid it for a long time, but every time I opened
My Eyes

   —looked in a mirror
      you know.

I decided to tell
Everyone
first my friends, they said they
Always Knew . . .
then my family, they were
Surprised

   —maybe its just
      a phase

I sat my parents down, opened
My Eyes
Lifted the lids so very
Slowly
Why not hide it, shut my eyes and
Stay Blind

—I will not deny
who I am

—John G. de la Parra, Jr.

SLICKER

came in a pink,
orange and white
striped metal tube,
with a black curlicue
border and a splayed
gold base. It came
in any number of
mod shades: Nippy
Beige, Chelsea Pink,
Poppycock, Hot Nec-
taringo, Pinkadilly,
Dicey Peach. There
were several tubes in
my mother's makeup
drawer in the bath-
room five out of six
of us used (my father
had his own bathroom,
as forbidden as the
walk-in closet where
his Playboys were
hidden under a stack
of sweaters on the top
shelf). All the girls
at school had Slicker
in their purses; I
watched them apply
The London Look
at the beginning and
end of each class. I
marveled at what else

spilled out: compact,
mascara brush, eye
shadow, wallet, troll
doll, dyed rabbit's
foot, chewing gum,
tampon, pink plastic
comb. At home I
stared at myself in
the medicine cabinet
mirror and, as my
brother pounded
on the locked bath-
room door, twisted
a tube and rubbed,
ever so slightly,
Slicker on my lips.

—David Trinidad

If We Were in a Gregg Araki Movie

If I were in a Gregg Araki movie,
I'd be the character who doesn't fit in. It's likely
like last night, when we watched the Doom Generation
I for a third or fourth time and you for the second in one night.
the first viewing had you alone and disturbed quite profoundly,
you had to get out of the house, you looked like you were crying,
called me. at first it didn't sound like you
I looked like I was happy to hear from you, watching it again
with you sounded like something to do.
I could come over, swim, or watch another movie,
but we watch the Doom Generation again.
First you had to pick up your girlfriend, at eleven
film at twelve. you have to drive her car
to the white room of the Grill for a child's Hot Dog plate
but you get it with fake Hot Dogs. It comes with Fries
You're another couple who have found me
the boyfriend you are jokingly claims
I'm ruining my chances with you, because of something
I've done I don't remember
My ex-boyfriend's been coming on to you. Oh, really
I know this is just your idea of playful, joking, little asides
We are going to watch the Doom Generation again
later, together. and why does it matter to you which character
I find more attractive, the one more like me, or the one more
like you? which do you?
or is it the character he's playing I find sexy?
I don't remember. I haven't seen it in a while. I'll go with
the second. I just remember liking that scene where
he's such an outcast sexually, abnormal and all, and
perfectly all right with it.
but maybe I'm already modifying my tastes to your discretion.

I get relish on my fake Hot Dog.
I'll still go home alone, but no yet.
First we get back in the car, I get in the back,
like at the beginning of the film, like the character I'm
identifying with. but only because he doesn't identify
with anybody, just bodies.
The three of us sit on the couch with your girlfriend in the middle,
just like the final climatic sex scene in the Abandoned Warehouse
with a bed, only we stay dressed. and I've never slept with
your girlfriend. she has to pee at exactly the same time as
the girl between the guys on the screen. gets up to leave
me and you to our own devices. we pause. two undressed men
look at each other, on hold. relish the moment. I'd be more like
the innocent one now.
your girlfriend asks what's the matter. am I beginning to
sympathize too much with this part? we could act this
entire movie out, but she's joking.
I'm miles ahead of the game.
The two of you inevitably fight,
while I'm waiting to bum a ride home
Your girlfriend and I are like the two at the end, because
we leave you there while she drives me home.
I was less sexually repressed in terms of you.
Add soundtrack, dialogue, roll credits.

—Douglas A. Martin

CRUSH

That boy
The wrinkles on his football jersey
Are more intriguing than geometry
Oh to reach over my desk
To smooth them out
Oh to make a page out of his back
And write my name just under his
Or over it
Squeezing in my letters between his
Locking them in place like hands weaving fingers
I can see him now running out into the stadium
Our names stitched together
A chorus of I LOVE HIM, HE LOVES ME
But wouldn't you know it?
That quarterback is unavailable
I've seen him speeding off after a game
His boyfriend in the car
Gathering each letter with a possessive arm

—Rigoberto González

ODE TO DJ

I'm in the mix, and the mix is in me

I don't really know him, but he knows me
Gets inside my deepest cell like DJ DNA
See he's got the key:
Double helix, rhythm, sound-
Deep House epiphany

And He,
He plays me

The night is his body, and the DJ, he's a gene
Can make down go up
And mix up all that's in between
He's the funk that through the green fuse drives the flower

Black light and dark, broken dirt of the night
DJ pushes me like green grass from the soil, born and waving like
a snake
into the sky
Pops a flower or two
Grows a goatee of twined bodies sexing in the night

And the freeway that arcs over these dancefloors
Busy bridges of sound changing lanes
He brings them all down
To spiral through the sex and the psychedelic psychology
Swimming in the green vines of his mulch and mix
Enwrapping me and rapturing
A symphony of who knows what and never heard again
These tunes of his are once upon a time

As are we all

And He,
He plays me

He's grown me into a tree
I'm a heaping pile of mashed potato cumulus clouds
Moved by his stormy, slippery hand
Mixing up the weather
—he makes me rain
He's windy, the sound of gravity and speed

And He,
He's moving through me

He's the chromosomic code that makes me hip-hop
Defines my everchanging form:
A blade of grass, a vine, a tree, a cloud-driven, weatherbeaten sym-
phony

He's the source and the sun
And the axis of the earth
—He makes it spin
And mixes you with me
In a congenital dance of ecstasy

And he—
He's a divine thing

So, when the night comes down like rain
There's a bass line splatter on the street
The world's a grease-gone gutter full of noise
Echoing his stormy message from the sky,

From the sea
From the river come back around
And come on back to me

It's in the mix
And the water like the music never ends

—Trebor Healey

FORM A BAND, GODDAMMIT

Real rock and rollers have ugly teeth and fucked-up hair
Everybody hates them at LMN Corporate School of Square
Their lockers get banged shut, resounding with 'Queer' 'Slut'
'Cumrag'
'Cunt' 'Prick' 'Fuckhead' 'Needledick' 'Twat' 'Douchebag'
'Bitch' 'Cocktease' 'Ballbuster' 'Pussy' 'Faggot'
'Lesbo' 'Homo' 'Cocksucker' 'Wussy' 'Maggot'
'Asshole' 'Asswipe' 'Piece of shit'
'Good-for-nothing worthless twit'

I need demonized guitars like I need skin and sky
Not pretty, not cool, titty cheerleaders, nor big-balled jocks
Future porn stars can kiss my ass and fuck American Pie
What they can't do is take their inner monsters from the box
Put them on the table, till they can stand with absolutely dreadful
pluck
Rise, fly—as only you real freaks can—form a band worth a fuck

—Horehound Stillpoint

DOUBLETALK

Fuck
portraying
the sun's

Why don't you paint

"petals of light."
Make something
darker, or fun

and shut your mouth

—the remains
of a moment;
sheen of our sweat . . .

and I'll kiss it

after Jack Spicer (1925–1965)

—Francisco Aragón

UNCERTAIN GEOMETRY

Tonight I curl my tongue around the uncertain
geometry of us; what pattern   might move us now
beyond the shaping of words, the tentative   touching
of teeth to tongue sculpting air into sound fluttering
like trapped birds through my ribcage—frightened
and foolish with hope   our borders will soften and shift

—Rita D. Costello

LILAC

There are sunsets I would've
written for you, this one
just
one more with you walking into it,
the other way
on Christopher St.
But this time it is real
and you don't even know
the color.

Three years
ago those streets
were still new and I
visited you to test the small
cavity, the recess of
desire somewhere after Bleeker
where we ate pizza and talked
about a boy you loved who
was too young to
know better, but still
you let him
in.

And would discretions
such as these
lend themselves more
to the Spring
where I never found you
Pruning the lilac bushes
in the field across
from my parents' home

what colors I strained
to clip, these violets
that streaked the sky across
your face as you said goodbye
Would I ever look more
beautiful to you,
even with the sun
in my eyes and the city
behind me?

—Brad Daugherty

CRUISING A HUNGRY WORLD

It is the season of meat.
Your dropped eyes would dissuade the passion
if they could. I lean in to inhale each breath
you make. You sense dark squirrels in my blood
and don't want me detecting any interest
from the banter and shifting soil

of our friendship: a flower afraid of soil;
a cage of ribs, suspicious itself of meat.
My press is driven less by fever than interest.
You try to counter what you perceive as passion,
try to forgive the garishness of my blood.
I'm not holding my breath.

Heading into my next breath,
I haven't a clue how soil
first rose up into tributaries of blood
to fill a tongue, setting in motion a dialogue between meat
and a hank of cloud. I'm not sure passion
is the residue of an excited star. That would probably interest

you. Harmonics and game strategies interest
you. You appreciate the spells a slight breath
can cast. For now, you channel your passion
the way a good farmer mounds soil
along a rivulet of water; no meat
floats red, raw, and sun-washed through the blood

of your narrow slough. Perhaps its danger in the blood
that I revere. You veer through subjects of interest,
though none takes. I smile a nail-pinning-meat
smile. You sigh, frown, and catch your breath.
I am a persistent rivulet that breaks the soil
you've just put in place. How aggravating passion

can be when it's not your mill churning the passion.
Loosen up. I'm only indirectly out for your blood.
Actually, I'm after something else. I'm coursing the soil
of another river moving carefully with interest
along a breeze of crises. My turn for a breath.
I'm already an ear up against a door of meat.

More than passion, my circles are those of interest.
Between us, bait is not blood; though breath
too can easily soil. I'm drawn to you as river, not meat.

—Scott Hightower

SERIAL TOXIC TEEN

the sidewalks ooze but are forgiven
31 slabs of iron in the basement for workout
boy on boy is okay
the sins are not the sins
forget what you are told
the guys in the confessional are wrong
the underworked think
that they are always overworked
and love comes no matter
emaciated websites peep at her cookies
thieves break into the mall and the
insurance premium increases
cuz of your youth
fiction is bottomless when telling the truth
it gets better

—Matthew Wascovich

PLAYING FOR LOVE

We drew a line with chalk rock across blacktop in the afternoon,
the neighborhood lined up and the curb crumbling.
"love-love," I called out,
the sunburn concealing our secret.
The game was on—
to keep the ball moving. We tangled rackets,
arms, legs, fell beautiful for a second, until we redirected,
drawing the heat from pavement against our knees
up to our hands and out
against each other.

When the streetlights flickered on,
the line was still visible, glowing.
Footprints and tire tracks would take days,
the kids would follow me for weeks
along with your eyes.

I remember
when we were older
playing the court at the part—
a real net, finally, and we were alone.
"love-love."
But then, there was no one
to cheer, no leaping the net.
Dust from vacant ball diamonds
blew hot across asphalt.

I remember walking home,
our rackets loose at our sides
knocking softly together.
"love-love."

And still when I say it, the hollowness of that sound
comes back: love as zero, full of possibility, waiting to be filled.

—Amanda R. Evans

I Got Beat Up A Lot in High School

He says. He smiles. He's sweet,
has become a lovely, gentle person.
I probably provoked them a lot,
he says. He's still small and sensitive.
There were lots of pregnancies, he says,
and suicides. The would drive off
a cliff in their cars, he says, just outside
of Blissing, Montana. And one girl,
he says, didn't know that her car
had airbags and she survived the impact
against the boulders on the bottom.
When she finally came back to school,
they said she could never do anything right,
Or they'd shoot themselves.
The all had gun racks on their pickups,
he says. Everyone drank quite a bit.
There was one gay bar, he says, where once
he saw his statistics teacher, soused,
and trolling for sex. But that's the past,
he says, sighing, sanguine and philosophic.
Now, I live in New York City, he says,
surrounded by friends and I can't conceive
of what I must have felt back then.
I'm sorry, I say, for all this pain in your past
and wrap my arms around his beautiful body.
It's not your fault, he says, and smiles,
looking out from inside himself.

—Christopher Murray

You Can't Go Back to Sleep

that year it was like everyone i knew fell out of a tree, hurt
themselves recklessly for show, a display of wringing limbs,
self-conscious origami of appendages that seemed suddenly new
and necessary, as if we'd just received these parts, just learned
that there were unknown things they might do, other uses
suddenly possible
plausible, i follow you on your bike through the path you
choose—twisting
dirt alleys and ditch bridges, i sensed the weight of them then—
arms and legs held
together by the stringy heat of sinews and muscle, straining,
straining to hold a course
to follow you to the field behind the baseball diamond, the heat
there a vacuum
and let you insist that this was actually my idea, the way we hide
our bikes in a shallow gully, sneaking through trash and weeds,
taller, more sure
than us, until we come to a spot where the grass is pushed flat by
other bodies, other kids
come to smoke pot and drink stolen beers
we are alone here, and you might motion then
that we lay down, maybe me on top of you, our faces not touching, not kissing, not looking
at each other, slipping hands underneath clothes, into them
placing our mouths on places other than mouths, our movements
a mimic of something
we can only guess at, until after several minutes, slick, uneasy, you
say stop
ok, you say, ok. there is a wave passing over us, a wind
of smothering, a thick breeze, we dress and shake this off, don't
speak, move back to our bicycles, our action figures, our endless

streets, sidewalks
driveways, and vague ideas—the heats and stirrings, the hint of
what we want
and wonder if everywhere in that warmth everyone else is waking
fumbling in bedrooms and bathtubs, at sleepovers and in tents,
backyards,
and under blankets, fingers moving moving and moving
while the streets spread out, heat hazy and limitless, bodies
become
slowly aware of themselves, uncalibrated instruments, the wheezes
and honks they produce, the uncontrolled bellows, the cacophony
a not so secret language—the clamor of singing parts—
of hips, hands and curious palms, shoulders, thighs
and suddenly upturned flesh, a chorus of hungry noises
that will soon resemble a tune, a summer song
we will eventually recognize as our own

—T. Cole Rachel

About the Editors

T. Cole Rachel grew up in rural Oklahoma, but now lives in New York City. Aside from writing poems, Cole makes a living as a magazine writer. After receiving a B.A. in English from Southwestern Oklahoma State University and an M.F.A. in Creative Writing from Wichita State University, Cole ran away to the big city and has never looked back. His work has appeared in *The Ontario Review, Lodestar Quarterly, A&F Quarterly*, and *Visionaire*. His previous book, *Surviving the Moment of Impact*, was published by Soft Skull Press in 2002. Later that year he was named Poet of the Year by *Inscape* and his collection of poems was hailed by TimeOut NY as "sweet-hearted, funny, idealistic and full of promise."

Rita D. Costello grew up on an island in the Niagara River, but has since lived in numerous cities throughout New York, Ohio, Kansas, Louisiana and now China—where she holds a joint position with Fort Hays State University in Kansas and SIAS International University in China. For much of her life, she focused her energy in the visual arts. Though literature and writing have since taken precedence, she keeps in touch with the visual arts through photography and various personal projects. Rita received her B.F.A. in Creative Writing and English from Bowling Green State University in Ohio, her M.F.A. from Wichita State University in Kansas, and her Ph.D. from the University of Louisiana in Lafayette. She has published poetry, short stories, and visual art in numerous journals including: *Fireweed, The Baltimore Review, Seattle Review, Illuminations*, and *The Slate*. Awards include the T. Reese Marsh Prize and 1st place in the *Glimmer Train* Poetry Open. Her scholarly interests are primarily in drama, film, politics and literature (especially literature of/about HUAC and the McCarthy era, genocide, and the Holocaust), gay and lesbian (or more broadly, alternative sexualities) literature, and interdisciplinary humanities.